1

W9-AFE-470

A12901 668786

Donated by

Mary Strong

© DEMCO, INC. 1990 PRINTED IN U.S.A.

I.C.C. LIBRARY

Decorating Baskets

I.C.C. LIBRARY

Decorating

Baskets

20 ORIGINAL AND
PRACTICAL GIFTS
FOR THE HOME
AND GIFT-GIVING

EMMA HARDY

I.C.C. LIBRARY

PHOTOGRAPHY BY GLORIA NICOL

LAUREL
GLEN

San Diego, California

TT
157
.H336
2003

Laurel Glen Publishing
An imprint of the Advantage Publishers Group
5880 Oberlin Drive, San Diego, CA 92121-4794
www.laurelglenbooks.com

Copyright © Cico Books, 2003

Copyright under International, Pan American, and Universal Copyright Conventions. All rights reserved.
No part of this book may be reproduced or transmitted in any form or by any means, electronic or
mechanical, including photocopying, recording, or by any information storage-and-retrieval system,
without written permission from the copyright holder. Brief passages (not to exceed 1,000 words)
may be quoted for reviews.

All notations of errors or omissions should be addressed to Laurel Glen Publishing, Editorial Department,
at the above address. All other correspondence (author inquiries, permissions, and rights) concerning the
content of this book should be addressed to Cico Books Ltd, 32 Great Sutton Street, London, UK,
EC1V 0NB.

Library of Congress Cataloging-in-Publication Data

Hardy, Emma.
  Decorating baskets : 20 original and practical gifts for the home and gift-giving / Emma
Hardy ; photography by Gloria Nicol.
    p. cm.
  ISBN 1-59223-007-5
  1. Handicraft. 2. Baskets. 3. Decoration and ornament. 1. Title.

TT157 .H336 2003
745.5–dc21   2002192701

1 2 3 4 5 06 05 04 03

Editor: Sarah Hoggett
Designer: Christine Wood
Photographer: Gloria Nicol

Contents

Introduction

Baskets come in all shapes and sizes, from brightly colored raffia or plastic shopping baskets to shallow straw bowls and chunky log and laundry baskets woven from willow. They make perfect storage containers and come in so many different styles and finishes that they can look good in every room of the house.

Baskets are not only ideal for storage, but they also make wonderful presents, too—both as a container for gifts and as a gift in their own right. If you've spent time choosing or making something special, then you want to make sure it's presented as attractively as possible. Baskets are the perfect way to present a gift and, unlike wrapping paper, they can be kept and used for many years to come.

But why stop there? With a little thought and imagination, you can transform even the most ordinary basket into something really special—and that's what this book is all about.

This book contains a host of simple, inexpensive ideas, using materials readily available from craft stores, that you can use throughout the year to decorate baskets for every occasion. All the projects can be created from start to finish in an afternoon.

Some of the projects are functional, quick-and-easy ideas that you can use to brighten up your own home, such as the stylish Pinecone Log Basket to spice up your hearth (page 72) and a neat little Sewing Basket with coordinating pincushion (page 78). Others, such as the stunning Copper-Leaf Table Decoration (page 54) and the Christmas Basket adorned with sparkling baubles (page 86), are decorative items in their own right.

On special occasions, decorated baskets really come into their own. The ideas featured here include pretty Wedding Baskets to take the place of the traditional bride's and bridesmaids' bouquets (page 42) and a Baby Shower Basket to give to expectant parents (page 16). And of course, the book contains a host of ideas for gifts to give to those special people in your life—a Mother's Day Planter (page 12), a Picnic Basket for those lazy, hazy summer afternoons (page 32), and colorful Trick-or-Treat Baskets for the kids at Halloween (page 58).

So enjoy making these projects and take inspiration from them, adapting the designs in your own way to suit the occasion. Your family and friends will be thrilled to receive such lovingly crafted, personalized gifts.

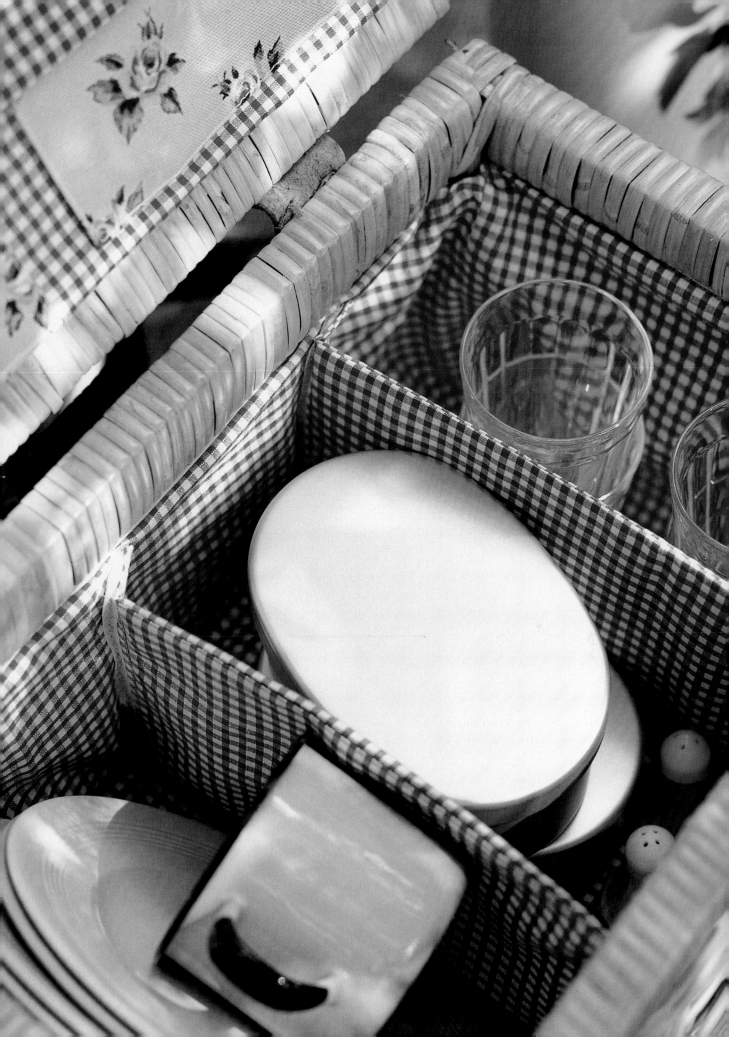

Spring

Lavender basket

Quick and easy to create, this elegant basket is suitable for all your storage needs and can even be used as a vase for a dried-flower arrangement. Made from inexpensive natural materials, its simplicity is the key to its success—just an elegantly shaped straw basket and stems of sweet-scented, purple lavender. Select a basket from your local garden supply store in the size you need. Pick the lavender stems from your garden, or use a bunch of dried stems: weaving with fresh stems will create a wonderful spring centerpiece, while dried stems will last throughout the year.

Materials

1 cone-shaped, natural
straw basket,
6½ in. high and 6 in.
in diameter

approx. 330 stems of
fresh or dried lavender

small pointed scissors

small hole pick

bottle of wood glue

1 Using the scissors, trim each lavender stem to approximately 2 in. in length. Using the hole pick, gently pry apart the fibers of the basket and slot each stem into the straw weave. Ease the stems in at an angle so that the lavender flowers stand out diagonally from the basket.

2 When you have completed one row, apply a line of glue to the inside of the basket and gently press the stems down into it. Allow it to dry for a few minutes or until the flowers are firmly fixed in place.

3 Repeat the first two steps, working up the basket row by row. When you have finished, trim away any excess stem pieces inside the basket and allow to dry overnight.

Mother's Day planter

Transform a simple wooden basket into a pretty planter that your mom will adore. Fill it with her favorite spring plants or flowers in her favorite colors to make a personalized gift that will last much longer than a bouquet. Lining the basket with plastic will protect the wood from water damage and help to retain moisture in the soil, keeping the plants looking good long after Mother's Day is over. Painting the basket with eggshell paint gives it a protective finish; use soft, pastel colors that coordinate with the flowers. Adding a layer of carpet moss and a pretty bow lends a professional-looking decorative touch.

Materials

shallow wooden basket,
approx. 11 x 8 x 9 in.

eggshell paint and paintbrush

16 x 12½ in. plastic sheeting

scissors

staple gun and staples

flowering plants of your choice

pottery shards or pebbles

potting compost

carpet moss

24-in. length of 1½-in. ribbon

1 Make sure the basket is clean, dry, and free from dust. (If the wood is untreated, paint the planter with a coat of primer.) Cover the planter with a coat of eggshell paint and allow to dry. Apply a second coat if necessary.

2 Cut a piece of plastic sheeting large enough to line the planter, adding an extra 1 in. all around. Fold the sheeting over by ¾ in. on each side and staple it to the inside of the planter, pleating it at the corners to form a neat lining.

3 Soak the plants with water before planting them. Place drainage material such as pottery shards or pebbles in the planter. Fill the planter halfway with potting compost and place the plants in position, filling in around the edges with more compost. Cover the surface of the compost with carpet moss.

4 For a pretty, decorative finish, take a 12-in. length of 1½-in. ribbon and tie a neat bow at the base of the handle on each side.

Baby shower basket

The best gifts for expectant parents are often the most practical, and this linen-lined basket would make a lovely gift at a baby shower. For a truly special present, fill it with baby-care essentials such as a beautiful blanket, hooded towel and washcloth, baby creams, and clothing—not forgetting baby's first teddy bear. Pockets in the lining, made from classic ticking fabrics, make the perfect easy-to-reach storage spot for lotions and creams, and they look pretty, too. The basket can also be used in the nursery as a stylish toy basket.

Materials

linen basket with
handles, approx.
21 x 16 x 10 in.

tape measure

1¾ yd. striped fabric

scissors

sewing machine

needle and thread

soft pencil

small pieces of colored
ticking for pockets

8 large, heart-shaped,
wooden buttons

1 Using the template as a guide (see page 93), measure the length of the basket, including the ends, both inside and out. Measure the width, add 3 in., and cut the striped fabric to this size. Lay the fabric out, right side down. Measure the length of the base of the inside of the basket and mark this along the center on both edges of the fabric. Make snips at these points 1 in. deep. Fold over the edges by ½ in. and then by another 1 in. and hem, leaving raw edges along the central part of each side.

2 Measure the long sides of the basket, inside and out, and cut two pieces of fabric measuring this length by the width of the unhemmed section of the long strip, plus a 3 in. seam allowance. Turn over by ½ in. and then by another 1 in. and hem along the two long sides of both pieces.

3 Right sides together, sew the side panels onto the unhemmed section of the long piece.

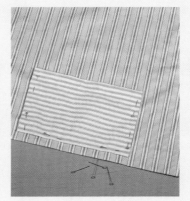

4 Mark the position for the handle slit with pencil marks on the wrong sides. Cut carefully as indicated and hem neatly.

5 Cut four ticking rectangles measuring 6 x 10 in. and hem the top of each one. Fold and press over ½ in. along the three remaining sides. Pin one rectangle to each side of the basket lining to make the pockets, and sew in place.

6 Cut four 5 x 6 in. pieces of ticking, fold in half lengthwise, and stitch ½ in. from the raw edge along one end and the length. Turn right way out. Turn under the remaining end, topstitch, and press. Sew the flaps onto the lining and attach a heart-shaped button at each corner.

Cockleshell basket

Pretty cockleshells around the rim give this charming bathroom basket a seashore theme that is complemented by the basket's color. It is practical too, as it is made from woven plastic, which is waterproof and will withstand humid conditions. Fill it with soaps and toiletries, a bath brush, and a natural sponge, adding one or two beautiful shells to make a gift suitable for both men and women. When the contents have been used up, the basket will make attractive bathroom storage. Try different shapes and colors of shells and a range of basket sizes to create unusual storage units for towels, washcloths, and toiletries.

Materials

colored plastic basket,
approx. 10 in. square

bradawl

hand drill with ⅛-in. bit

50 cockleshells in varying sizes

galvanized wire

wire cutters

1 Make a hole in each shell using a bradawl. Place the shell on a solid surface and drill a hole with the hand drill, pressing down firmly.

2 Cut a length of wire approximately 16 in. long. Wire the end onto the basket, twisting it around itself a couple of times to hold it securely. Thread a large shell and then a small shell onto the wire and fasten the wire through the basket to hold the shells firmly in place.

3 Continue adding shells, alternating the sizes and fastening the wire through the basket after every two shells to secure them.

4 Continue to wire the shells onto the basket until the rim is covered. Twist the wire through the basket rim several times and trim the end to give a neat finish.

Materials

twiggy basket approx. 8 in.
in diameter and 5 in. high

25–30 quails' eggs

sharp needle

saucer or bowl

glue gun with glue sticks

1 yd. gingham ribbon

decorative Easter chick

1 Pierce both ends of the quails' eggs with a sharp needle, then move the needle carefully around inside the eggs to break up the yolk. Gently blow out the yolks and egg whites. Wash the eggs in mild water and detergent solution and allow to dry standing on end, so they can drain.

2 Using the glue gun, start to glue the quails' eggs onto the rim of the basket. Arrange the eggs in small clusters of three or four, varying the angles slightly.

3 Continue to glue the quails' eggs onto the basket rim, creating a pleasing arrangement.

4 Cut four lengths of gingham ribbon approximately 8 in. long and tie them in neat bows. Glue the bows at regular intervals around the rim of the basket, between the clusters of eggs. To complete the decoration, glue a pretty Easter chick onto one of the eggs on the basket rim.

Summer

Beach basket

This brightly colored shopping basket would make a great gift for a friend or loved one planning a vacation. Fill it with a beach towel, sandals, books, and well-chosen maps and guidebooks to help her make the most of her trip. The bright colors evoke feelings of lazy summer days. The basket can be used for trips to the beach or for sightseeing—a welcome reminder of your good wishes for an enjoyable vacation.

Materials

brightly colored shopping basket, 13½ x 6 x 9 in.

nylon jewelry thread

approx. 250 colored beads

needle

scissors

1 Thread a needle with nylon jewelry thread and fasten the end onto the basket by making a few small stitches. Sew on a bead, sewing between the weave of the basket to avoid damaging it. Sew on another bead approximately 2 in. from the first in the same way.

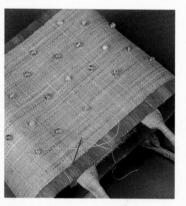

2 Continue to sew beads onto the basket, spacing them evenly and varying the colors to make a pretty arrangement. Cover the front and back of the basket, leaving the sides bare.

3 Thread the needle with more nylon thread and tie a knot in the end. Thread six beads, all the same color, onto the thread.

4 Sew the string of beads onto the basket just under the rim and tie it off firmly inside the basket. Continue to fringe around the basket, ensuring that the end of each thread is held securely in place.

Picnic basket

Take the comforts of your own dining table outside with this stylish, attractive, and easy-to-make picnic basket. Line it with classic gingham embellished with pretty floral fabrics and decorative buttons. With simple dividers to organize all the essentials for a perfect outdoor picnic and pockets for cutlery and other utensils, this basket will be used over and over again on those special summer days. Use plastic cups and plates for a durable and hard-wearing hamper or, as we did, glass and china for more distinguished picnic parties.

Materials

hamper-style basket
with lid, approx.
22 x 13 x 12 in.

tape measure

5 ft. red gingham

scissors

sewing machine

needle and thread

11½ ft. of
1-in. Velcro

glue gun and
glue sticks

cardboard

scraps of floral fabric

4 buttons

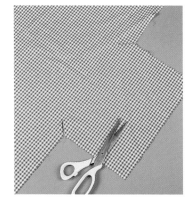

1 Measure the inside of the basket, add 1½ in. all around, and cut out a piece of gingham to this size. Cut out the corners, adding a ¾-in. seam allowance to each side of the flap of material left on the short end of the fabric. This will create neat corners, so that the lining fits snugly inside the basket.

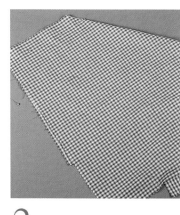

2 Sew the corners together, stopping 1½ in. before you reach the top on all corners. Press open the seams.

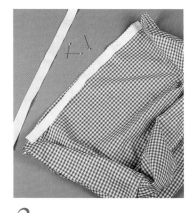

3 Fold the raw edges of the lining over to the wrong side by ¾ in. and again by another ¾ in. and press. Pin and stitch a strip of Velcro along each edge. Glue the corresponding Velcro strips inside the basket and allow to dry. The Velcro holds the lining firmly in place inside the basket.

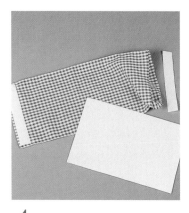

4 For each divider, cut a piece of cardboard the width of the basket. Cut two gingham pieces 1½ in. wider and 3 in. longer than the cardboard. Right sides together, taking a ¾-in. seam, sew along three sides. Turn right side out and press. Stitch Velcro along the closed end of the pocket and stitch underneath it. Insert the card and stitch below it. Fold in the raw ends by ¾ in. and stitch Velcro to the back. Sew the corresponding Velcro pieces to the lining.

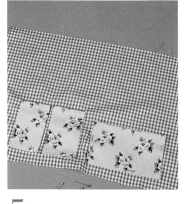

5 Cut a piece of cardboard to fit inside the lid of the basket and two rectangles of gingham 1½ in. wider and 3 in. longer than the cardboard. Cut rectangles of floral fabric and hem along one edge. Turn under the raw edges and stitch onto one of the gingham rectangles, leaving the hemmed end open. Cover the cardboard as for the dividers.

6 Sew Velcro to each end of the panel front. Glue corresponding strips inside the lid. Cut a 4-in. strip of gingham the width of the panel plus 1½ in. Fold in half widthwise, right sides together, and stitch around three sides, taking a ¾-in. seam. Turn right side out; press. Turn under the raw edges and hand stitch to close. Sew buttons onto the strip and glue onto the lid panel. Velcro the panel to the lid.

Girl's gift basket

This delightfully decorated gift basket would grace any young lady's dressing table. There is no sewing involved: the braids are simply glued in place. For a little girl, fill the basket with hair accessories, pretty soaps and bubble baths, and glittery jewelry. For a teenager, you might opt for makeup and toiletries. If you want a bit of Hollywood-style glamor, strings of sparkly sequins or pretty, pastel-colored feathers would make a glitzy alternative to the braids.

Materials

colored basket, 4½ in. high and
7½ in. in diameter

4 x 24-in. lengths of braid in varying
colors and widths

craft glue

scissors

1 Measure and cut a length of braid to fit around the rim of the basket. Applying glue in small sections, stick the braid onto the basket. Make sure the end of the braid is glued down firmly.

2 For the second length, choose a wider braid. Glue it onto the basket in the same way as the first, making sure that it is an even distance from the first braid all the way around.

3 Take a third braid the same width as the first, and glue it around the basket to create a border effect.

4 Finish the decoration with a fourth strip of braid, again making sure that it is positioned the same distance from the previous braid all the way around. Allow to dry completely before you fill the basket with gifts.

Button basket

A charming addition to a plain sewing table or a decorative and useful gift for the needlewoman in your life, this button basket can be created in less than an hour. All you need are cast-off buttons or trimmings from other projects and a plain basket with a lid. You can either keep to a single color theme, such as the shades of white and cream used here, or mix and match. Green and blue or red and pink would both work well against the natural color of the straw. For a brighter, fun look, use a selection of trimmings. Try multicolored beads, paillettes, or sequins.

Materials

closely woven undyed straw basket with
flat lid, approx. 3½ in. high and 5½ in. in diameter

approx. 150 assorted buttons or other trimmings

button thread or strong waxed cotton in
matching color

embroidery needle

1 Making sure your basket is clean and dry, practice the pattern you want to make on the basket with your buttons, positioning large buttons first and filling in the gaps with smaller ones. Now sew buttons onto the lid of the basket.

2 Keeping the thread loose and pulling the needle through the weave of the straw to avoid damaging it, sew the remaining buttons onto the body of the basket.

Wedding baskets

This florist's basket filled with fresh flowers, the handle beautifully bound with satin ribbon, makes a delightful change from the traditional bride's or bridemaid's bouquet. Use blooms in a single color that coordinate with the color scheme of the wedding and frame them with simple foliage. Choose seasonal flowers to complement the bride's dress or stick to classic roses, cramming in as many as the basket will hold for an abundant look. A piece of florist's foam soaked in water and placed in the bottom of the basket will keep the flowers fresh throughout this most special of days.

Bride's basket

Materials

florist's basket lined with plastic, approx. 9 x 6 x 4¾ in.

1 can of cream-colored, craft spray paint

old newspaper

a block of florist's foam to fit inside the basket

2 yd. of ½-in. satin ribbon for the handle

needle and thread

sprigs of green foliage

pruning shears

15–20 fresh roses

2 yd. of 1½-in satin ribbon for the bows

1 Working in a well ventilated area, spray the basket with cream paint, covering your work surface with newspaper to protect it. When the basket is completely dry, place the block of florist's foam inside it. Wrap the satin ribbon around the handle, overlapping it slightly to give an even coverage and stitching the ribbon to itself in places to secure it. When you have completely covered the handle, secure the end of the ribbon with a few small stitches.

2 Pour water onto the florist's foam to wet it thoroughly. Cut the stems of the green foliage leaves to about 2 in. long and push them into the florist's foam all around the rim of the basket, overlapping each leaf slightly. Use slightly smaller leaves on either side of the handle to give it a neater finish.

3 Using a pair of sharp pruning shears, cut the rose stems at an angle to about 2 in. in length, carefully removing any thorns. Starting from the middle of the basket, push the roses into the florist's foam. Use smaller blooms around the edge and to fill any gaps. When the basket is full, complete the decoration by tying a pretty satin ribbon bow on either side of the handle.

Bridesmaids' baskets

These two basket ideas, the larger one suitable for the bridesmaids and the smaller one ideal for a flower girl, can add to the joy and beauty of the occasion. Again, the baskets can be made to coordinate with the wedding outfits, either using tiny bunches of artificial flowers of similar colors on a cream basket, or spray-painting the basket a suitable color. Silk linings can transform even quite basic and inexpensive baskets into something extra special. Fill the baskets with paper confetti or dried rose petals for the bridesmaids to shower over the happy couple as the ceremony draws to a close.

Materials

baskets with handles,
approx. 8 in. high and
6½ in. in diameter

white spray paint

old newspaper

pale green spray paint

¼ yd. cream silk and
matching thread

tape measure

scissors

pins and needle

sewing machine

imitation flowers on wires

approx. 8 ft. of ½-in.
satin ribbon

1 Working in a well-ventilated area, spray the basket with white paint, covering your work surface with newspaper to protect it. This is a good base when using a colored paint, as it will give a more solid paint finish.

2 When the base coat of paint has dried, spray the basket with green paint, giving additional coats if necessary to create an even coverage. Allow the basket to dry completely.

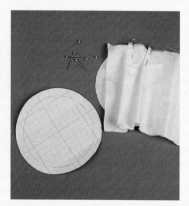

3 Measure the inside base of the basket and cut a piece of silk to fit, adding a ¾-in. seam allowance all around. Cut another piece of silk the circumference of the basket plus 12 in. by the height of the basket plus 1½ in. Pin and stitch the side panel to the base, pleating it slightly as you go. Pin and stitch the side openings together.

4 Press the lining and turn the top over by ¾ in., making sure that the pleats are straight all the way around. Pin and baste to hold the pleats in place.

5 Place the lining inside the basket and stitch it firmly in place, pushing the needle through the holes in the weave to avoid damaging the basket.

6 Arrange the flowers around the rim of the basket, twisting the wire through the basket to hold them in place. Turn the basket around as you work to make sure that the arrangement looks good from all sides.

7 Use the same method to make a smaller cream basket for the flower girl. To finish, bind a length of ribbon around the handle as for the bride's basket and tie a neat bow at either side of the handle.

Fall

Basket decorated with rags

For a traditional homespun look, this open basket interwoven with gingham scraps makes a charming laundry basket. The perfect gift for the homemaker, fill it with scented linen waters (ideal for scenting laundry), muslin bags filled with rose petals or lavender stems bound with ribbon, and practical cotton cloths. It will be a welcome addition to any laundry room. Alternatively, use it as a bread basket as part of a rustic table arrangement or for a summer lunch *al fresco*.

Materials

basket, approx. 8 in. high and 13½ in. in diameter

12 in. of three or four gingham fabrics that work well together

bradawl

1 Tear strips of cloth that are about 1–1½ in. wide and long enough to weave once around the basket. Tie a small knot in one end of each one.

2 Using the bradawl to make a hole in the weave, push the fabric through from the inside of the basket to the outside. Push the fabric back through the basket about 1 in. farther along. Continue until the fabric strip has been woven around the basket. Repeat with different fabrics all the way up the basket, staggering the rows.

3 Tear 7-in. strips to decorate the rim. Fold each strip in half lengthwise and push it from the inside of the basket to the outside ¾ in. from the top. Pull the ends of the fabric through the loop and tighten, leaving the ends sticking up. Cover the whole top in this way, spacing the strips about ½ in. apart.

Copper-leaf table decoration

Oak leaves, so abundant in fall, make an ideal motif for this delightful centerpiece for a homey dinner party. The leaves, which are cut from a thin copper sheet, contrast beautifully with the woven basket, and a layer of sumptous carpet moss introduces another pleasing texture. Fix candle pins (available from craft stores) into the basket or make your own, following the instructions on page 56, making sure that they are securely in place before you insert the candles. Never leave lit candles unattended and always extinguish them well before they burn down to the level of the basket.

Materials

plastic-lined table basket,
12 in. in diameter and
1½ in. high

candle pins or metal
confectioner's tins, nails, and
bradawl

copper wire

carpet moss

paper for template

sticky putty

1 pack of sheet copper

soft pencil

scissors

tracing wheel

glue gun with glue sticks

3 gold candles

1 If you are using candle pins, glue or wire them onto the bottom of the basket. To make your own, make a hole in the center of the base of a confectioner's tin with a bradawl and push a nail through the hole from the underside. Make two more small holes in the base of the tin, push through a short length of copper wire, and twist it tightly through the weave of the basket to hold it in place.

2 Place pieces of moss in the basket, pushing small pieces around the candle holders. Make sure that the moss is packed in tightly and that none of the plastic lining can be seen.

3 Use the template (see page 92), or draw an oak-leaf template on paper, and cut it out. Place it on the sheet copper and, using a piece of sticky putty to hold it in place, draw around it with a soft pencil. Carefully cut it out with sharp scissors. Make enough copper leaves to fit around the basket.

4 Using a tracing wheel, mark veins on the copper leaves. Cut one 4-in. length of copper wire for each leaf. Bend the end of each wire over to make a small loop and glue it onto the back of each leaf using a glue gun.

5 Push the wires through the basket, twisting them around themselves to hold firmly in place. Overlap the leaves slightly and vary the angles to make an attractive arrangement. Wire leaves around the hole in the center of the basket and push gold candles into the holders.

Trick-or-treat baskets

Transform plain and utilitarian galvanized buckets into cheery trick-or-treat baskets to help set the scene for a ghoulish Halloween. Cover buckets in thin, textured papers, embellish them with autumnal leaf shapes cut from colored papers in russets, oranges, browns, and greens, and fill them with candies to hand out to visiting trick-or-treaters. Alternatively, let each child decorate his or her own bucket and use it to collect treats. The motifs around the top of the buckets could include pumpkin shapes, bats, black cats, and moons and stars.

Materials

galvanized metal
bucket, 5½ in. high
and 6½ in. in diameter

thin colored paper

scissors

clear tape

craft glue

4½ ft. green gift
ribbon

pencil

cardboard

colored construction
paper in autumnal
shades

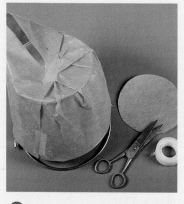

1 Cut a piece of colored paper long enough to go around the bucket and wide enough to be tucked into it and gathered at the base. Fix the paper in place with clear tape and fold the top of it into the bucket, taping the paper to the inside of the bucket. Make small snips and cut out a section around either side of the handle.

2 Turn the bucket upside down, carefully gather the paper into pleats, and tape it in place. To finish the base neatly, cut a disc of paper slightly smaller than the base and glue it in place over the pleats.

3 Line the bucket with another piece of paper slightly shorter than the bucket. Glue it around the top and hold it in position for a couple of minutes until it adheres firmly.

4 Tape the end of the gift ribbon to one side of the handle and wind it around the handle, making sure there are no gaps. Tape the other end in place. Cut a length of ribbon and, holding one blade of a pair of scissors, carefully pull the ribbon over the blade to curl it. Tie the ribbon curl around the base of the bucket handle and trim. Repeat on the other side.

5 Use the template (see page 92), or draw a leaf shape on cardboard, and cut it out. Using the cardboard shape as a template, draw around it on colored construction paper and cut out leaf shapes. Score the leaf pattern onto the leaves using the sharp end of the scissors, and bend the leaves slightly to make them look more three-dimensional.

6 Glue the paper leaves around the bucket, varying the angles and overlapping them slightly. Continue around the bucket until all the leaves are stuck on.

Birthday basket

Brightly colored ribbons are used to great effect here to create a cheerful party basket that is perfect for holding favors to give to guests. Simply thread short lengths of plain and gingham ribbons in candy colors around the rim of a colored wicker or raffia basket. Then make small cones from colored and patterned wrapping papers, fill them with candies or lollipops, and place them in the basket ready to hand out to guests as they leave. For a more sophisticated gathering, such as a wedding or Christmas dinner, you could use ribbons in more muted tones and fill the basket with sugared almonds wrapped in white or silver paper.

Materials

colored wicker or raffia basket, approx. 12 x 10¼ x 4 in.

40–50 12-in. lengths of colored ribbon in varying colors and widths

scissors

1 Cut the ribbons to lengths of approximately 12 in. Make them slightly longer than they will need to be so that you can trim them if necessary when they are all in place.

2 Fold a length of ribbon in half and, using the scissors to make a small gap in the weave of the basket, push the loop under the rim from the inside of the basket to the outside. Pull the ribbon ends through the loop and tighten.

3 Continue to loop the cut lengths of ribbon through the basket, varying the colors and widths of ribbon as you go.

Dried flower basket

A basic willow basket becomes a beautiful
table decoration when it is adorned with
carefully preserved dried flowers. Pick
flowers from your own garden and dry
them in an airing cupboard for an especially
individual gift, choosing favorite blooms to
evoke happy memories of shared times in
the garden, or use store-bought dried
flowers and foliage in colors to complement
the recipient's home. Dried flowers will
make a floral focus that will last all year
long. You can use colors of a similar palette
or, as in this version, opt for a more lively
look by adding a single bright bloom.

Materials

shallow willow basket,
11 in. in diameter

30–40 dried colored oak leaves

glue gun and glue sticks

12 small dried
hydrangea heads

10 small bundles dried marjoram

florist's wire

8 dried achillea heads

12 seed heads

1 Make small bundles of oak leaves with four or five leaves to a bundle and glue them onto the basket, loosely covering the rim. Overlap the leaves slightly.

2 Cut clusters of hydrangea florets in small heads and arrange the heads between the leaves. When you are completely happy with the arrangement, glue them in place.

3 Cut marjoram into 3½-in. lengths and bind them together in bundles with florist's wire. Push the stalks into the basket weave, again securing them with glue when you are happy with their position.

4 Complete the arrangement with brightly colored achillea flower heads and seed heads. Fill any spaces with the remaining flowers and glue them in place.

Pet basket

The perfect gift for animal lovers, this cozy pet basket will be loved by cats and dogs alike. Made from soft, fleecy fabric, the lining can easily be removed for washing. We decorated the fabric with a cute bone design. Choose a fish or mouse motif for a cat or, for an even more personalized basket, cut the pet's name from cream fleece and sew it onto the cushion. Make a soft fabric shape to attach to the basket, and your pet's favorite toy will never go missing again!

Materials

Woven dog basket, approx. 29 x 19 x 8in.

piece of foam for the cushion, 1 in. thick

approximately 1 yd. green fleece fabric

10 in. cream fleece fabric

10 in. fusible webbing

matching thread

synthetic stuffing

30 in. cream cord

green tapestry thread or yarn and tapestry needle

1 Cut out two large bone shapes from cream fleece fabric. Pin them right sides together and stitch around the edge, leaving an opening of about 1½in. Turn the bone the right way out.

2 Fill the bone with synthetic stuffing. Insert one end of the cream cord about 1 in. into the opening, and hand stitch the opening closed. Using a tapestry needle and green tapestry thread or yarn, blanket stitch around the edge of the bone.

3 To line the sides, pleat and pin a piece of paper around half the basket to make a curved shape. Cut out two pieces of green fleece using this pattern piece. Pin and stitch the two pieces together to make one long strip and press open the seam.

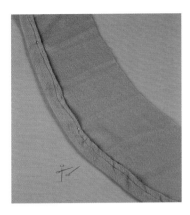

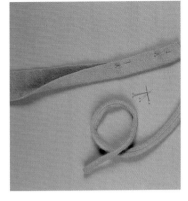

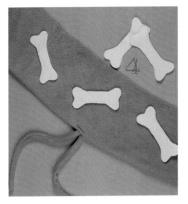

4 Fold over the top edge by ½ in. and machine stitch in place. Fold this edge over again by 1¼ in. and hand stitch neatly in place.

5 To make ties to hold the lining in place, cut two 26 x 2½ pieces of green fleece, fold them in half lengthwise, and pin and stitch one short end and the long, raw edge. Pin a large safety pin to the stitched short end and feed it back through the inside of the tube to turn it the right way out. Press. Fold the ties in half and machine stitch onto the basket lining.

6 Following the manufacturer's instructions, iron fusible webbing to the back of the cream fleece. Draw a small bone shape on paper and cut out your pattern. Cut 10–12 bones from the cream fleece. Peel off the backing paper and position the bones on the basket lining. Lay a damp cloth over the bones and iron them to fix the bones in place. Machine stitch the bones in position. Lay the lining inside the basket and pin and stitch the ends together. Stitch the cord on the toy bone to the lining.

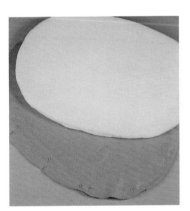

7 To make the cushion cover, cut out two oval shapes from green fleece the same size as the foam cushion plus 1¼ in. all around. Taking a ¾ in. seam, stitch the ovals together, leaving an opening of about 6 in.

8 Turn the cushion cover the right way out and insert the cushion. Hand stitch the opening closed. Pin the lining for the basket sides around the top of the cushion and machine stitch. Place in the basket, and tie the ties through the basket weave to hold the lining in place.

Winter

Pinecone log basket

Quick to make and very effective, this sturdy pinecone log basket will make a welcome addition to any hearth. Collect pinecones on long country walks and simply wire them on. The perfect gift for weekend hosts, the basket can be filled with logs ready to burn or with dried orange peel, bundles of lavender, and fir branches to give off a delightful scent by the heat of the fire. Make newspaper twists and include bundles of kindling and matches for the complete fireside companion.

Materials

sturdy log basket

florist's wire

wire cutters

30–40 pinecones

1 Cut lengths of florist's wire about 8 in. long. Push one wire through the bottom of each pinecone and twist it around the base once or twice, leaving 5–6 in. free. Wire enough pinecones to fit all the way around the top of the basket.

2 Push the wire through the basket from the outside, working with the weave to avoid damaging the basket. Pull the wire all the way through so that the pinecone sits snugly on the basket. Wrap the wire over the top of the basket and push it through to the inside again, pulling it tight. Wind the wire around itself under the pinecone and snip off the end to neaten.

3 Continue to wire the pinecones onto the basket, with some facing inward and some facing outward to give a more interesting look, until you have covered the whole rim.

Bread basket

There is no nicer gift than a homemade one, and a basket of freshly baked muffins is a particularly welcome offering. To make it even more special, a stylish, linen basket liner can be made with flaps to tie up over the muffins to keep them warm. Here, a classic striped linen fabric has been used with plain linen on the other side to make a reversible basket lining that can be used again and again. This bread basket is an attractive addition to a breakfast setting and indispensable on a picnic for keeping bread and baked goods fresh. For a real treat, a traditional muffin recipe is included on page 77.

Materials

shallow basket with handles,
12 x 9 x 6 in.

tape measure

pattern paper and pencil

scissors and pins

36 x 32 in. striped linen fabric

36 x 32 in. plain linen fabric

1 yd. of ½-in. linen ribbon

needle and thread

clear tape

sewing machine

1 Using the template (see page 93) as a guide, measure the base of the inside of the basket and the depth of the two short ends and draw a rectangle on paper to these dimensions. At each end, mark a triangle that is just over half the width of the basket in height. Add a ¾-in. seam allowance all around, pin the pattern to the striped fabric, and cut out. Make two triangles the width of the basket base along their long side and just over half the width of the basket in height, and a rectangle to fit each side of the basket, with the stripe of the fabric running vertically. Pin the triangular pieces to the long fabric piece.

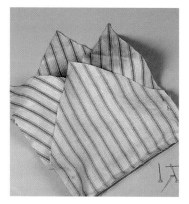

2 Pin and stitch the corners of the lining together, stopping ¾ in. short of the top at each corner. Press open the seams.

3 Lay the two triangular pattern pieces onto the main pattern piece, overlapping the seam allowance along the bottom, and tape in place. Pin the pattern onto the plain linen and cut out.

4 Stitch the corners together, stopping ¾ in. from the top of each corner. Press open the seams.

5 Lay the striped lining right side up on the table and pin the plain linen lining on top of it, right side down. Cut four lengths of linen ribbon and pin one at each corner between the two layers, making sure they are pinned within the seam allowance. Stitch the two pieces together, leaving an opening about 4 in. long along one straight side. Trim the seam allowance. Turn the lining the right way out and press. Hand stitch the opening, and place the lining in the basket.

Blueberry Muffin Recipe

1½ cups plain flour

¼ cup sugar

2 tsp. baking soda

¼ tsp. salt

2 eggs

8 tbsp. melted butter

¾ cup milk

1 tsp. vanilla extract

1 tsp. grated lemon rind

¾ cup fresh blueberries

Heat the oven to 400°F. Sift the flour, sugar, baking soda, and salt into a bowl. Whisk the eggs until blended in a separate basin, then add the melted butter, milk, vanilla, and lemon rind, then mix well. In the bowl of dry ingredients, make a small well and slowly pour in the egg mixture. Lightly stir the mixture until the flour is coated, but not until the mix is smooth. Fold in the blueberries with a metal spoon. Spoon the batter into the cups of a buttered and sugared muffin pan; do not over-fill the cups. Bake for 25 minutes or until the muffin tops spring under your touch. Cool in the pan for a few minutes, then turn out. Serve warm.

Sewing basket

A traditional sewing basket is the perfect gift for someone with a passion for needlework, and is quick and easy to make. Pretty floral fabric with a retro feel is used to make a lining with customized pockets to keep the tape measure, scissors, and thimble close at hand, leaving plenty of room for a selection of spools of thread, ribbons, and other sewing tools. Ties around the handles hold the lining in place, making a practical and charming gift with a homey feel.

Materials

tape measure

deep basket with handles, 12 in. in diameter

30 in. floral fabric and scraps of coordinating
fabric for pockets

needle, pins, and thread

scissors and pinking shears

sewing machine

1 Measure the base of the basket and add ½ in. all around. Cut out a circle of fabric to this size. Cut out a rectangle of fabric long enough to fit around the inside of the basket, adding about another third of this measurement for the pleats, and deep enough to fold over the edge of the basket by about 2 in. Add 2 in. for seam allowance. Right sides together, pin and stitch the rectangle to the base piece, making small pleats all the way around.

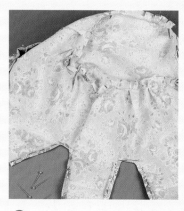

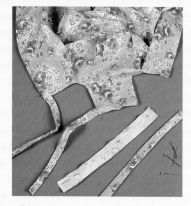

2 Place the lining inside the basket inside out and mark the position of the handles with pins. Carefully snip the fabric to the pins. Take the lining out of the basket. Fold over the raw edges around the handle slits by about ¼ in., fold over again by ¼ in., and pin and stitch in place. Press.

3 Cut eight 2 x 8 in. pieces of fabric. Fold lengthwise, right sides together, and stitch the long side ½ in. from the raw edge. Trim the seam allowance to ¼ in. Turn right way out and hand stitch the raw ends to close. Press. Fold over the raw edge of the lining by ½ in. and then again by another ¾ in. Pin the ties into the folded hems at the handles. Stitch in place. Hand stitch the hem.

4 To make the pockets, cut small rectangles using pinking shears and pin them onto the basket lining. Sew the pockets in place with neat topstitching. Press the lining and place it in the basket.

Patchwork pincushion

A pretty addition to the sewing basket is a lovely patchwork pincushion. Made from scraps of cloth in coordinating colors, it couldn't be cheaper to create. Use floral fabrics for a bright and lively look, or stick to traditional gingham for a more homespun feel.

Materials

tape measure

scraps of pretty fabrics

sewing machine

needle, thread, pins

stuffing

pencil and paper
for template

scissors

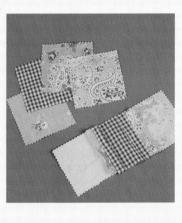

1 Measure and cut nine squares of fabric about 3½ in. square. Lay them out and move them around until you're happy with the arrangement. Use gingham fabrics next to florals and space out the solid colors. Taking a ½-in. seam allowance, pin three pieces together. Repeat with the remaining squares to create three strips of cloth.

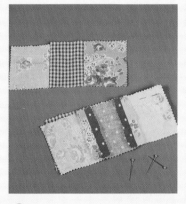

2 With right sides together, pin and stitch the three strips together to make a square. Press open the seams.

3 Use the template (see page 92), or draw a heart shape on paper, adding ¼ in. seam allowance all around and cut out. Pin the heart shape to the patchwork panel and cut it out. Cut out another heart shape from a single piece of fabric. Pin the two hearts right sides together. Stitch together, taking a ¼-in. seam allowance and leaving a 2 in. opening along one side. Trim the seam allowance and make small snips around the rounded parts.

4 Turn right way out and press. Fill the heart with stuffing and then hand stitch the opening to complete the pincushion.

Rosemary basket

This beautifully aromatic basket is a great way to thank a hostess after a dinner party. The fresh herbs not only look and smell attractive, but can be used by your hostess in subsequent feasts. Choose a rustic-style basket and decorate it with bundles of fresh rosemary. Bay leaves, lavender, or any fresh herbs would work well and would be a welcome addition to a cook's kitchen. The herbs will continue to look attractive as they dry out and fresh herbs can be added as necessary. Fill the basket with crackers and breadsticks, wrapped in cellophane for freshness, and include tasty cheeses as an extra special gift.

Materials

rustic basket, approx. 9 x 10½ x 9 in.

100–120 sprigs fresh rosemary

scissors

florist's wire

wire cutters

24-in. length of ½-in. gingham ribbon

1 Cut small pieces of rosemary about 3 in. long. Bind four or five sprigs together just below the end by wrapping a short length of florist's wire around them. Make enough rosemary bundles to cover the basket rim.

2 To fasten the bundles to the rim, push the wire through the basket and twist it around itself several times to secure each bundle in place. Snip off any excess wire at the end.

3 Continue to wire the rosemary bundles onto the basket, overlapping them slightly to make an even arrangement. Finish off the basket by tying a bow of gingham ribbon at either side of the handle.

Christmas basket

Transform a classical, wire garden urn into a dazzling festive gift basket. Add sleek silver, glimmering glass, and glittering baubles for that up-to-date festive feel. The basket could be an alternative to the traditional Christmas stocking, perhaps for adults. Or, fill it with a selection of small after-dinner gifts and make it part of your annual Christmas decorations. Keep the colors cool and icy for a sophisticated feel or use bright metallics and colored ribbons for a fun, lively look. After the holiday period, simply take off the baubles and put the basket back in the garden for another year.

Materials

urn-shaped wire basket,
approx. 14 in. high and 12 in. in diameter

clear nylon thread

scissors

20–25 x 2-in. clear baubles

35–40 x 1-in. matte silver baubles

5 yd. of 2-in. organza ribbon

1 Cut lengths of nylon thread and tie them onto the clear baubles. Tie the baubles around the rim of the basket, finishing with a couple of knots to hold them securely in place.

2 Tie two or three smaller, silver baubles together to make clusters. Tie the clusters onto the basket above the clear baubles, varying the sizes for a more random look. Continue around the basket.

3 Tie loose bows of organza ribbon onto the basket, spacing them evenly around the rim and leaving lengths of ribbon hanging down the sides.

Gift wrapping

When you were a child, did you ever surreptitiously pick up your presents from under the Christmas tree and shake and prod them to try and guess what was inside them? Perhaps you still do! But wrappings are not only used to add suspense and excitement, they can also be beautiful in their own right.

Whether you are presenting a whole basket as a gift or simply using it as a container for smaller gifts and favors, there are countless wrapping options open to you. The traditional method of wrapping with paper and finishing with a ribbon tied in a bow offers an infinite number of permutations. Try mixing bright colors together for a modern, fun look; use metallic papers and ribbons for a Christmasy feel; or try pastel-colored papers tied with gingham ribbons for a gentle, feminine touch.

And there are just as many ways to embellish your gift wrappings. For a sophisticated and smart look, use ribbons the same color as the wrapping paper; or try a utilitarian look, teaming brown parcel paper with brightly colored ribbon or string. For a more extravagant idea, tie two colors of ribbon together around a present and finish with a large bow. For extra decoration, attach a fresh or an artificial flower to a package or tie on bundles of fresh herbs and spices, such as cinnamon sticks or star anise, with colored braid.

If the gift is unusually shaped—a bottle, for example—gift boxes and bags are a great solution. Decorate them with beautiful ribbons, and try adding beads and buttons for a more creative finish. Or make your own containers: take inspiration from the Birthday Basket (page 62) and make paper cones to hold gifts of candy and chocolate.

Wrapping presents in cellophane can also be very effective. Simply gather up a large piece of cellophane around the present and tie it with a big bow and ribbon curls. This type of wrapping is particularly suitable for large gift baskets; the gift can still be seen, but thought and effort have obviously gone into the presentation.

For a completely different approach, try wrapping gifts with part of the present. Tie a pretty linen dishcloth around a selection of kitchen gifts, a special napkin around homemade cookies or breads, or a delicately embroidered handkerchief around some scented soaps. Gifts such as the charming Mother's Day Planter (page 12) are not suited for wrapping, and so a well-chosen ribbon will do just fine.

There are wrappings to suit every taste and to cater to every occasion, in a huge range of colors, patterns, and textures. But with just a little effort, you can create personalized and original gift wrappings that will show just how much you care.

Templates

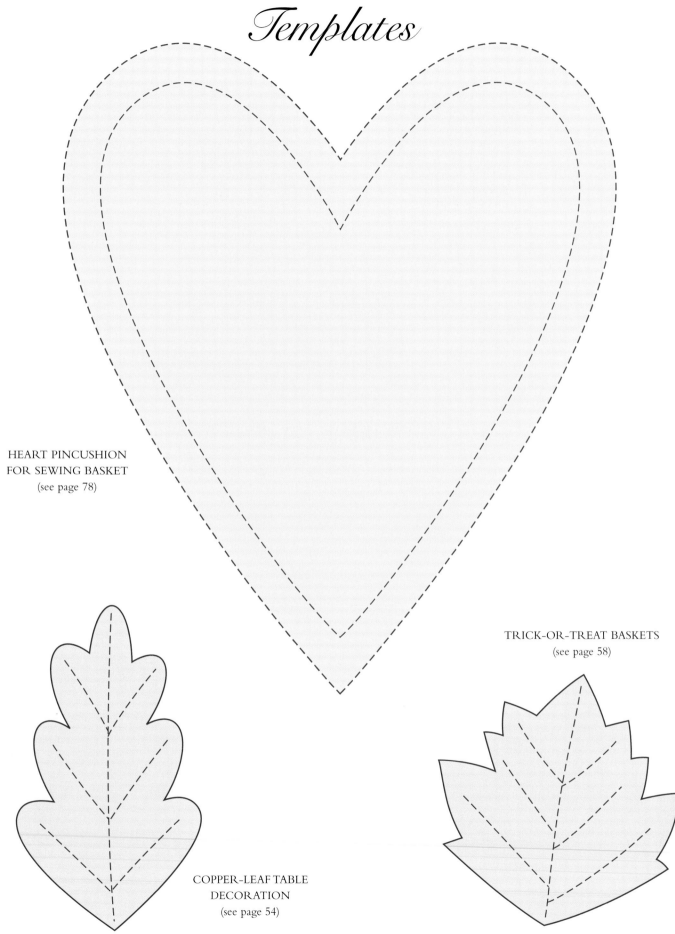

HEART PINCUSHION
FOR SEWING BASKET
(see page 78)

TRICK-OR-TREAT BASKETS
(see page 58)

COPPER-LEAF TABLE
DECORATION
(see page 54)

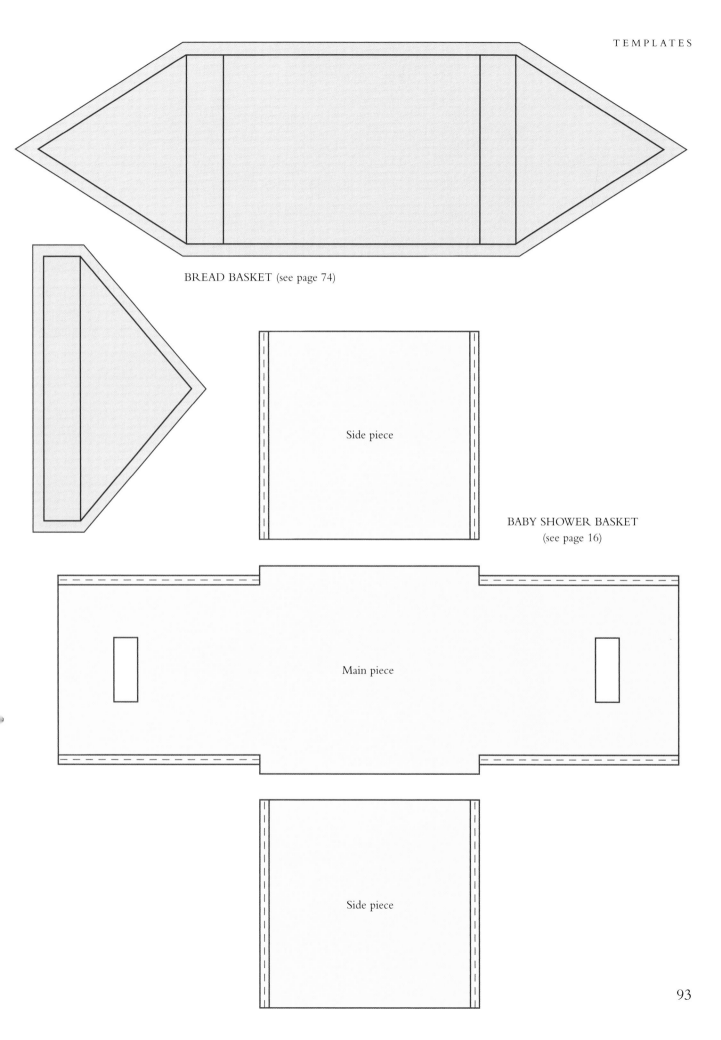

BREAD BASKET (see page 74)

Side piece

BABY SHOWER BASKET
(see page 16)

Main piece

Side piece

Techniques

HOW TO CHOOSE THE RIGHT BASKET

Baskets are available in a wide range of shape, sizes, and materials. When choosing a basket to give as a gift, there are several things to bear in mind. Choose a basket with a style in keeping with the gift or event. Baskets made from hazel, willow, woven twigs, and branches create a homespun, traditional feel and are well suited to projects using fresh and dried herbs and foliage. Baskets made from reeds and paler woven leaves have a fresh, simple, and natural look. Painted or dyed baskets come in a whole spectrum of colors; they are ideal for children's gift baskets and add a fun note to party decorations. Or choose wire, galvanized buckets, or woven plastic for a modern, contemporary feel.

Choose the size of the basket according to the project, bearing in mind that the larger the basket the more will be needed to fill it. Go for baskets on the small side if they are to be filled with small items, as cramming the presents will give a more abundant look. Use a larger basket for larger items, such as logs for the fire, baby blankets and towels, and picnicware. Remember that the larger the basket, the more decoration it will need—so make sure that you have enough materials to decorate the project without skimping.

Baskets that are to be used solely for decoration will probably not need to have handles, but obviously baskets that will be carried or moved around will—so this will also influence your choice. Simple florist's baskets with a single long handle work well for bride's and bridesmaids' posies, while a traditional-style linen basket with a handle at each end will be suitable for a baby shower gift or similar practical basket.

CHOOSING THE WEAVE

The weave of the basket is an important thing to bear in mind when choosing a basket. Several of the projects in this book use a technique of pushing ribbon, fabric, or wire through the weave and so it is essential that the weave is fairly loose or can be pushed open slightly. If gluing braids or other decorations onto a basket, ensure that it is fairly flat and even or, as with the Easter basket (see page 24), that the decoration will sit comfortably around the rim. Baskets containing fresh flowers or moss will need to be lined with plastic to keep moisture in; these baskets should be made from a tight weave, or from a solid material such as wood, so that the lining will not be seen through the basket.

PREPARATION AND ESSENTIAL MATERIALS

Before starting any of the projects, make sure that you have all the materials you need, in the quantities that will be required. When painting a basket, ensure that the surface is smooth and dust free, and use a primer for a hardier finish. When using spray paint, always work in a well ventilated area, mask the whole area with newspaper or scrap paper, and wear a mask while spraying. With both spray paint and eggshell paint, wait until each layer is completely dry before applying another coat.

While the projects in this book are all fairly simple and do not require specialist craft materials, it is worth buying the following essentials: good craft glue; sharp dress-making scissors; paper scissors; a glue gun and general-purpose glue sticks. Wire cutters will also be useful for several of the projects ,as will gardening secateurs for the floral projects.

FINISHING TOUCHES AND TRIMMINGS

As with the materials, very few special craft techniques are used, although a basic knowledge of sewing will be useful. Unless otherwise stated, a seam allowance of ¾-in. is used throughout. When the seams have been sewn, trim the seam allowance to about ¼-in. to give a neat finish and make small snips around curved seams. Press the stitched fabric as you go for a smart look. When sewing beads and buttons, always sew from the inside of the basket to the outside to hide thread ends, and finish off with a few small stitches to hold the beads in place securely.

When gluing decorations onto baskets, choose a suitable glue, preferably a fast-drying one. Hold the decorations in place until the glue is dry and work slowly and methodically to ensure that the decorations have adhered well. Some decorations can be wired onto baskets; when doing this, wind the wire firmly onto the basket to hold the decoration in place and trim any long ends of wire, tucking the end into the basket.

There are many materials that can be used to decorate baskets, from ribbons, buttons, feathers, fabrics, and braids to more specialist materials such as sheet copper, baubles, and quail's eggs. For style with economy, collect natural decoration from country walks, such as dried flowers and pinecones; or use garden flowers and herbs.

Ribbons and bows can enhance a gift basket. Use a generous length of ribbon to make a pretty bow for a more lavish look. Wired ribbons are especially effective as they keep their shape well.

USING TEMPLATES

Five of the projects in this book require templates (see page 92). To use the templates, simply photocopy the shape required and cut out the photocopy. Enlarge or decrease the size of the template on the photocopier to make bigger or smaller shapes as necessary. Pin this template onto fabric (for the pin cushion) and cut out, or draw round the shape onto copper (for the oak-leaf table decoration) or onto colored card (for the trick-or-treat baskets).

Stockists

BASKETVILLE
8 Bellows Falls Rd.
Putney, VT 05346 US
Tel: (001) (800) 258–4553
www.basketville.com

COST PLUS WORLD MARKET
200 Fourth Street
Oakland, CA 94607 US
Tel: (001) (510) 893–7300
www.costplus.com

JO-ANN FABRIC & CRAFTS
841 Apollo St., Suite 350
El Segundo, CA 90245 US
Tel: (001) (888) 739–4120
www.joann.com

MICHAELS
8000 Bent Branch Dr.
Irving, TX 75063 US
Tel: (001) (800) Michaels
www.michaels.com

PIER 1 IMPORTS
301 Commerce Street, Suite 600
Fort Worth, Texas 76102 US
Tel: (001) (800) 245–4595
www.pier1.com

International and regional dialing codes are shown in brackets

Index